Axel Jörn

Does research pay?

An analysis of R&D expenditure and economic performance in small and medium sized enterprises

Anchor Academic
Publishing

Jörn, Axel: Does research pay? An analysis of R&D expenditure and economic performance in small and medium sized enterprises, Hamburg, Anchor Academic Publishing 2016

Buch-ISBN: 978-3-95489-450-5
PDF-eBook-ISBN: 978-3-95489-981-4
Druck/Herstellung: Anchor Academic Publishing, Hamburg, 2016

Bibliografische Information der Deutschen Nationalbibliothek:
Die Deutsche Nationalbibliothek verzeichnet diese Publikation in der Deutschen Nationalbibliografie; detaillierte bibliografische Daten sind im Internet über http://dnb.d-nb.de abrufbar.

Bibliographical Information of the German National Library:
The German National Library lists this publication in the German National Bibliography. Detailed bibliographic data can be found at: http://dnb.d-nb.de

All rights reserved. This publication may not be reproduced, stored in a retrieval system or transmitted, in any form or by any means, electronic, mechanical, photocopying, recording or otherwise, without the prior permission of the publishers.

Das Werk einschließlich aller seiner Teile ist urheberrechtlich geschützt. Jede Verwertung außerhalb der Grenzen des Urheberrechtsgesetzes ist ohne Zustimmung des Verlages unzulässig und strafbar. Dies gilt insbesondere für Vervielfältigungen, Übersetzungen, Mikroverfilmungen und die Einspeicherung und Bearbeitung in elektronischen Systemen.

Die Wiedergabe von Gebrauchsnamen, Handelsnamen, Warenbezeichnungen usw. in diesem Werk berechtigt auch ohne besondere Kennzeichnung nicht zu der Annahme, dass solche Namen im Sinne der Warenzeichen- und Markenschutz-Gesetzgebung als frei zu betrachten wären und daher von jedermann benutzt werden dürften.

Die Informationen in diesem Werk wurden mit Sorgfalt erarbeitet. Dennoch können Fehler nicht vollständig ausgeschlossen werden und die Diplomica Verlag GmbH, die Autoren oder Übersetzer übernehmen keine juristische Verantwortung oder irgendeine Haftung für evtl. verbliebene fehlerhafte Angaben und deren Folgen.

Alle Rechte vorbehalten

© Anchor Academic Publishing, Imprint der Diplomica Verlag GmbH
Hermannstal 119k, 22119 Hamburg
http://www.diplomica-verlag.de, Hamburg 2016
Printed in Germany

Table of contents

List of figures 9

List of tables 10

List of formulas 11

List of abbreviations 12

1 Introduction 13
   1.1 Task of assignment 13
   1.2 Basic information and thesis 13

2 Theoretical basis of innovation management 15
   2.1 Innovation management 15
   2.2 Methods to measure efficiency of innovation and R&D expenditure 17

3 Analysis of R&D expenditure of SME`s 19
   3.1 Analysis of all companies 19
      3.1.1 Ratio of profitability to weighted R&D expenditure 20
      3.1.2 Ratio of profitability to total R&D expenditure 22
      3.1.3 Ratio of cost structure to weighted R&D expenditure 24
      3.1.4 Ratio of cost structure to total R&D expenditure 26
      3.1.5 Ratio of cost structure II to weighted R&D expenditure 27
      3.1.6 Ratio of cost structure II to total R&D expenditure 29
      3.1.7 Mean value investigation: T-test for independent samples 30
   3.2 Analyses for companies which invest in R&D 32
      3.2.1 Ratio of Profitability to weighed and total R&D expenditure 32
      3.2.2 Ratio of cost structure to weighed and total R&D expenditure 35
      3.2.3 Ratio of cost structure II to weighed and total R&D expenditure 37
   3.3 Analyses for selected branches 39
      3.3.1 Medical devices industry 40
      3.3.2 Medical devices industry without outlier 43
   3.4 Results 45

4	Conclusion and outlook	48
4.1	Recommendation	48
4.2	Related Studies	49
4.3	Summary	50

List of appendices 52

List of references 53

List of internet references 53

Appendix 54

List of figures

Figure 1:	Classification of innovations.	16
Figure 2:	Scatter diagram: Correlation between weighted R&D spending and profitability	21
Figure 3:	Scatter diagram: Correlation between overall R&D spending and profitability	23
Figure 4:	Scatter diagram: Correlation between weighted R&D spending and cost structure	25
Figure 5:	Scatter diagram: Correlation between overall R&D spending and cost structure	26
Figure 6:	Scatter diagram: Correlation between weighed R&D spending and cost struct. II	28
Figure 7:	Scatter diagram: Correlation between overall R&D spending and cost structure II	29
Figure 8:	T-test for independent samples: Profitability by R&D expenditure	30
Figure 9:	T-test for independent samples: Profitability due to R&D personnel	30
Figure 10:	T-test for independent samples: Cost structure by R&D expenditure	31
Figure 11:	T-test for independent samples: Cost structure by R&D personnel	31
Figure 12:	T-test for independent samples: Cost structure II by R&D expenditure	32
Figure 13:	T-test for independent samples: Cost structure II by R&D personnel	32
Figure 14:	Scatter diagram: Correlation between weighed R&D spending and profitability	33
Figure 15:	Scatter diagram: Correlation between overall R&D spending and profitability	34
Figure 16:	Scatter diagram: Correlation between weighted R&D spending and cost struct.	35
Figure 17:	Scatter diagram: Correlation between overall R&D spending and cost struct.	36
Figure 18:	Scatter diagram: Correlation between weighted R&D spending and cost struct. II	37
Figure 19:	Scatter diagram: Correlation between overall R&D spending and cost struct. II	38
Figure 20:	R&D disbursements/revenue ratio of branches	39
Figure 21:	Correlation: Weighted R&D spending and profitability (medical devices)	41
Figure 22:	Correlation Overall R&D spending and profitability (medical devices)	42
Figure 23:	Correlation Weighted R&D spending to profitability (without outlier)	43
Figure 24:	Correlation: Overall R&D spending and profitability (without outlier)	44

List of tables

Table 1:	Thresholds of coefficient importance	21
Table 2:	Correlation matrix: Weighted R&D spending and profitability	22
Table 3:	Correlation matrix: Total R&D spending and profitability	23
Table 4:	Correlation matrix: Weighted R&D spending and cost structure	25
Table 5:	Correlation matrix: Total R&D spending and cost structure	26
Table 6:	Correlation matrix: Weighted R&D spending and cost structure II	28
Table 7:	Correlation matrix: Total R&D spending and cost structure II	29
Table 8:	Correlation matrix: Weighted R&D spending and profitability	34
Table 9:	Correlation matrix: Overall R&D spending and profitability	34
Table 10:	Correlation matrix: Weighted R&D spending and cost structure	36
Table 11:	Correlation matrix: Overall R&D spending and cost structure	37
Table 12:	Correlation matrix: Weighted R&D spending and cost structure II	38
Table 13:	Correlation matrix: Overall R&D spending and cost structure II	38
Table 14:	Figures of branches with the highest R&D/revenue ratio	40
Table 15:	Correlation matrix: Weighted R&D spending and profitability (medical devices)	41
Table 16:	Correlation matrix: Total R&D spending and profitability (medical devices)	42
Table 17:	Weighted R&D spending and profitability (without outlier)	44
Table 18:	Correlation matrix: Total R&D spending to profitability (without outlier)	44
Table 19:	Overall summary of correlation matrix results and interpretation	46
Table 20:	Overall summary of T-test results and interpretation	47

List of formulas

Profitability 20
Weighted R&D expenditure 20
Pearson's product- moment correlation coefficient 22
Cost structure 24
Cost structure II 27

List of abbreviations

R&D (FuE)	Research and development (Forschung und Entwicklung)
SME	Small and medium sized enterprises
LED	Light emitting diode
PM	Project management
NPV	Net present value
BC	Business case

1 Introduction

1.1 Task of assignment

In order to develop or protect competitive advantages, companies, besides other initiatives, increasingly invest more and more in research and development (R&D) to foster innovation and dynamic capabilities. Consequently, discussions about the effectiveness and benefit of R&D expenditure have become popular in the recent years.

This paper dealing with the topic, "Does research pay? -An analysis of R&D expenditure and economic performance in small and medium-sized enterprises (SME)-", was written in the second semester on the module of "Research Methods" to obtain a Master of Business Administration. In the first part, the theoretical basis for innovation management, calculation of benefit, evaluation methods of R&D initiatives in companies are given. The second part presents a quantitative analysis of the efficacy of R&D expenditure and economic performance of SME based on a data set produced from the Statistisches Bundesamt Germany and by using MS Excel the programming language "R". Finally, this assignment provides a summary, an outlook, and a recommendation for further research.

1.2 Basic information and thesis

The dataset is comprised of the cost structures and balance sheets of 500 German companies in the field of processing-trade and mining, indicating the branch of the economy, regional placement and other major economic figures, such as the number of employees, turnover, assets, energy consumption, deposits, wages and different kinds of costs, total added value, and R&D expenditure. The mining industry includes companies that are involved in excavating coil, turf, mineral oil, gas, uranium, metal ore, industrial stone, and minerals. The processing-trade companies are further divided into various types, e.g. nutrition, textile, leather, wood, paper, print, chemical, metal, stone and mineral, mechanical, electronic, medical, automotive industry, etc. The data is representing a smoothed and anonymized microanalysis.

The main weakness of this data is that it is a cross section investigation. A longitudinal section investigation would be much more appropriate for the problem at hand. Another weakness is the examination of an isolated point in time. In other words, if there is a relationship between R&D and a company's performance, we have to assume that the company did not have a different R&D investment in the past. In reality however, if a company invests today, it does not necessarily mean it did in the past. In such a case, the dataset would show R&D costs but the company's current benefits have nothing to do with earlier investments.

Nonetheless, this assignment seeks to locate for a positive relation between the revenue or profitability and cost structure in relation to R&D expenditure. It can be assumed that a company that invest in R&D may have better products that can be sold at a higher price. Consequently, such accompany must have a higher profitability. In addition, R&D investments could also lead to better production processes so that the same product could be produced at lower costs. Hence, we arrive the thesis that research pays and leads to a better company profitability. First, there will be analyses on all companies and companies who invest in R&D. Second, there will be a study of companies having dedicated branches.

2 Theoretical basis of innovation management

As R&D departments are mainly concerned with developing innovations, this section summarises the most important terminologies and fundamentals of innovation management in general. It also lists and introduces the different methods and instruments to measure the added value of R&D expenditure and economic performance.

2.1 Innovation management

Innovation means "something new" or "renew" and needs to be differentiated from the word invention. Invention implies an idea or a flash of inspiration and with that begins the first creative step of the whole innovation process, whereas innovation indicates the development of an invention to a mature and "ready for the market" solution, product, process or service. Indeed, the idea is an essential aspect of each innovation. However, it is almost useless without a proper practical context or adequate implementation.[1] A famous example is the light bulb. Seventy-one years passed between Humphry Davy, in 1809, connecting two wires to a battery and attaching a charcoal strip between the other ends of the wires, and Thomas Edison in 1879, taking a carbon filament that burned for forty hours and placing this filament in an oxygen free bulb. In 1991, Philips invented a light bulb that lasts 60,000 hours.[2] In 2015, other innovative technologies such as LED have disrupted the lighting market and might make the initial technical solution of a fervent wire negligible. An invention becomes an innovation if it brings useful performance or adds value.[3] According to the innovation-scientists Hausschild and Salomon, innovations can be technical (products, processes and knowledge), organizational (structures, cultures, systems and managerial), and business (renewing business processes, branch structure, market structure or the rules of the game).[4] Innovations can be divided into five dimensions. These are content (what is new?), identity (how new?), subjective (new for whom?), process (where does the innovation starts and end?), and normative (is it successful?). One can categorize an innovation as new for the organization and new for the market. The figure 1 represents this idea.

---

[1] Rf.: Amberg, M. (2010), pp. 111 - 112
[2] Rf.: HIL (2015)
[3] Rf.: Amberg, M. (2010), p. 112
[4] Rf.: Hauschildt, J. (2011), pp. 9 - 10

Figure 1: Classification of innovations.[5]

All products, services, or processes that fit into one of these categories, are innovations irrespective of their potential to bring value and diversity in the degree of novelty. To form an idea into innovation, enterprises implement an innovation process containing the four steps: idea search, idea selection, implementation, and evaluation. The related strategies can be divided into "market pull" and "technology push strategy". Another aspect connected to innovation and R&D is the distinction between open and closed innovation. Closed innovation means that only internal R&D of an organization is involved in the development, whereas open-innovation considers external partners like suppliers, customers, and even competitors. In recent years, open innovation has become more popular than closed innovation. All these attributes are important to answer the question of this assignment properly. There are several other terms (fuzzy front end), methods (degree of innovation), topologies, and possibilities to classify innovations, all of which cannot be explained, considered or determined in this paper.[6] As the authors want to give some recommendation at the end of this investigation, they assume that mature project management (PM) methodologies are deployed in the mining and processing sector to manage innovation.

---

[5] Rf.: Amberg, M. (2010), p. 113
[6] ibid, pp. 113 - 115

2.2 Methods to measure efficiency of innovation and R&D expenditure

The following paragraph deals with the measurement of the benefit of innovation and lists the different calculation methods. According to Schmeisser, there is a gap in scientific knowledge related to calculation methods to determine the success of innovation.[7] The practical statistics about the success of inventions (ideas) show the importance of measuring their sense and prosperity. An interdisciplinary, empirical, and long-term study into the ideas of 116 companies reveals that only 11 out of 1.919 are actually successful. Fewer than 10% of the ideas have entered the market. The market disclosed 70% of them as unsuccessful. From the remaining products, 46% were sold with deficit, 33% did not bring significant profit, and only 21% were finally successful and soled with profit.[8] There are different dimensions to the success of an idea or innovation. One can refer to the success of a project in relation to an innovation, or the total project portfolio of several innovation projects, or even on company level. As the given data set provides figures mirroring the overall performance of the companies and their related R&D spending, for this study a literature review of measurement methods for success at the company level was performed.

According to Schmeisser, the contemplation at the company level by using performance indicators like turnover, growth in turnover and revenue is difficult due to two reasons. Firstly, the success of a company is influenced by several other internal (degree of dynamic capability, innovation, ect.), and external (micro- and macro- environmental) factors. Therefore, there is no causal relationship between a successful innovation management and the success of a company. The second weak point of this approach is that the actual numbers for turnover, revenue, or income returns are based on the innovations or achievements of the past, which, therefore, give no evidence of the present innovation initiatives. Moreover, the success of the resulting product depends on factors like the related marketing mix, after-seals service, etc.[9] Consequently, the academic measurement of the success of innovations is done at project not at company level.[10] Nevertheless, this assignment approaches science at this stage by developing formulas and calculation models based on quantitative methods using MS Excel and the statistical analysis software "R" in order to determine the success of R&D spending

---

[7] Rf.: Schmeisser, W. (2008), p. 3
[8] ibid, p. 3
[9] ibid, p. 8
[10] ibid, p. 5

based on figures at the company level. The literature offers several techniques of measuring the value of innovations and R&D spending. These are:

- Rating and solvency check
- Technology cost analysis
- Technology balancing
- Technology portfolio matrix
- Target costing
- Berliner balance score card[11]

All these methods are used to answer the scientific question of this assignment using different methods and with several advantages and disadvantages. As none of these research models is applicable to the given dataset, a further description of these techniques is not needed.

---

[11] ibid, pp. 10 - 18

3 Analysis of R&D expenditure of SME`s

This section presents statistical analyses by applying several functions of the programming language "R". Based on the Excel data set described in section 1.2 the embedded "rcmdr-package" is used to answer the question "Does research pay?" The following "R" functions are applied:

- Regression analysis: Scatter diagram
- Descriptive statistical analysis: Correlation matrix (R^2)
- Mean value investigation: T-test for independent samples

With the first two functions, it is possible to identify whether there are any statistical connections between two or more variables in a sample, to understand how strong these connections are, and to test the probability that these relationships also exist within the whole population.[12]

The purpose of the T-test is to check whether the means of two variables differ significantly or not. As prerequisites, the variables must have a metric level and need to be normal distributed. In general, if the two resulting means of the variables are identical, then there is a zero hypothesis.[13]

As already stated, companies that invest in R&D may have the better products, that can be sold at a higher price which results in a better company profitability. Additionally, R&D investments could also lead to better production processes and lower costs and better gross value added. Therefore, the next paragraph seeks for evidences to prove the thesis.

3.1 Analysis of all companies

This paragraph at first, seeks to find a correlation between profitability and R&D expenditure using the scatterplot and correlation matrix function of "R". Secondly, it looks for a relation between cost structure and R&D spending. In the last part, a mean value analysis (T-test) is used to identify a relation and prove this thesis.

---

[12] Rf.: Zimmer, M (2015), pp. 160 - 164
[13] ibid, p. 187

3.1.1 Ratio of profitability to weighted R&D expenditure

At first, the profitability needs to be calculated. The profitability of a company involves how its revenues are related to the total costs. As profitability is not given in the original data set (Appendix 1), it must be calculated using the following formula:[14]

$$\text{Profitability} = \frac{\text{Total revenue}}{\text{Total costs}} \qquad (1)$$

The profitability can be found in column AK of the modified data set that is attached to Appendix 2 of this assignment.

Since it can be assumed that a bigger company may have higher R&D expenditure another important aspect is the analysis which uses the weighted R&D expenditure. Hence, the following formula needs to be introduced. This principle sets the R&D expenditure in relation to the total revenue.[15]

$$\text{Weighted R\&D expenditure} = \frac{\text{R\&D expenditure}}{\text{Total revenue}} \qquad (2)$$

The results of this calculation can be found in column AL of the modified data set in Appendix 2. The first investigation is a scatterplot shown in Figure 2. The green line is the least square criterion that represents a mathematical standard procedure to find a curve close to the data points in a data point cloud. This square criterion indicates that there is a relation between the weighted R&D spending and profitability.

---

[14] Rf.: Busse von Colbe, W. (2013), p. 194
[15] The formula has been developed by the authors

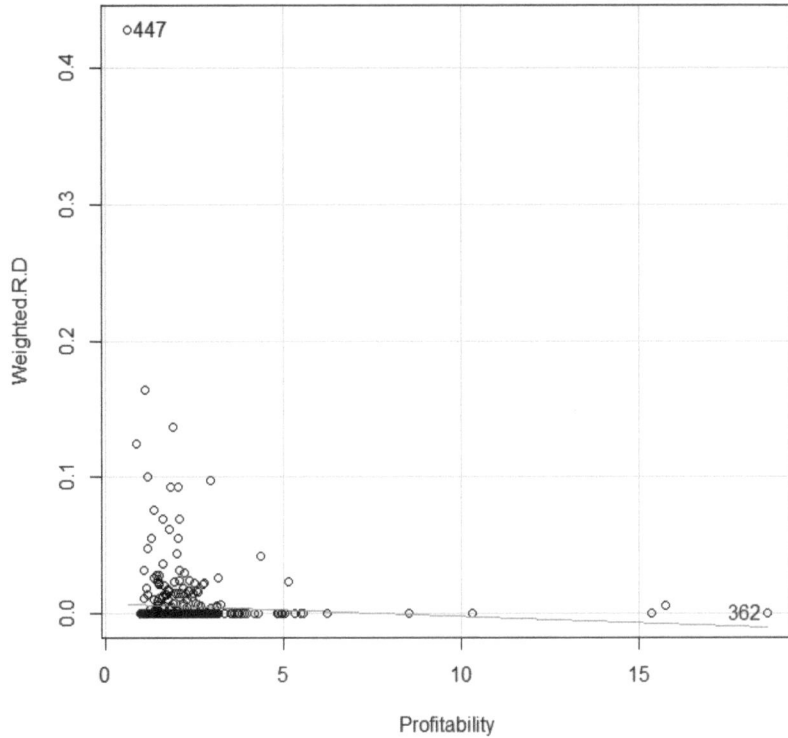

Figure 2: Scatter diagram: Correlation between weighted R&D spending and profitability

The next descriptive investigation is the Correlation matrix. The correlation between two variables is expressed with a coefficient that needs to be interpreted. As a rule of thumb, for correlations in statistical analyses in social sciences, the thresholds in Table 1 are applicable.

Coefficient	Importance of coefficient
<= 0.05	negligible
> 0.05 and < 0.2	low
> 0.2 and < 0.5	intermediate
> 0.5 and < 0.7	high
>= 0.7	very high

Table 1: Thresholds of coefficient importance[16]

---

[16] Rf: Fernandez, E. O. (2009): p. 7

The exact statistical method depends on the scale level of the variables. R offers two mathematical approaches. "Pearson's product-moment correlation coefficient" and "Spearman's rank correlation coefficient". As both variables have interval scales, the correlation was measured by means of "Pearson's product-moment correlation coefficient" using the following formulas:

$$r_{x,y} = \frac{S_{x,y}}{S_x \cdot S_y}$$

$$S_{x,y} = \frac{1}{n-1}\sum_{i=1}^{n}(x_i - \bar{x})(y_i - \bar{y}) \text{ (covariance)} \quad (3)$$

$$S_x = \sqrt{\frac{1}{n-1}\sum_{i=1}^{n}(x_i - \bar{x})^2} \; ; \; S_y = \sqrt{\frac{1}{n-1}\sum_{i=1}^{n}(y_i - \bar{y})^2}$$

If the coefficient is in the range of [-1, 1] the following rules are applicable.

+ 1 indicating a perfect positive linear relation

+ 0 indicating no relation

+ (-1) indicating a perfect negative linear relation[17]

Table 2 is shows the output of the descriptive statistical analysis "correlation matrix" function of "R".

	Profitability	Weighted R&D expenditure
Profitability	1.00000000	-0.05463883
Weighted R&D expenditure	-0.05463883	1.00000000

Table 2: Correlation matrix: Weighted R&D spending and profitability

As the coefficient is -0.054, there is a weak and slightly negative, hence negligible, correlation. Practically, it can be stated that there is no correlation.

3.1.2 Ratio of profitability to total R&D expenditure

Like the investigation above, this chapter examines the relation between profitability and total R&D expenditure. Course of this consideration is that companies may have to spend comparable costs for developing one new product or one new production process, regardless of the size or revenue of the company.

---

[17] Rf.: Zimmer, M (2015), pp. 161-164

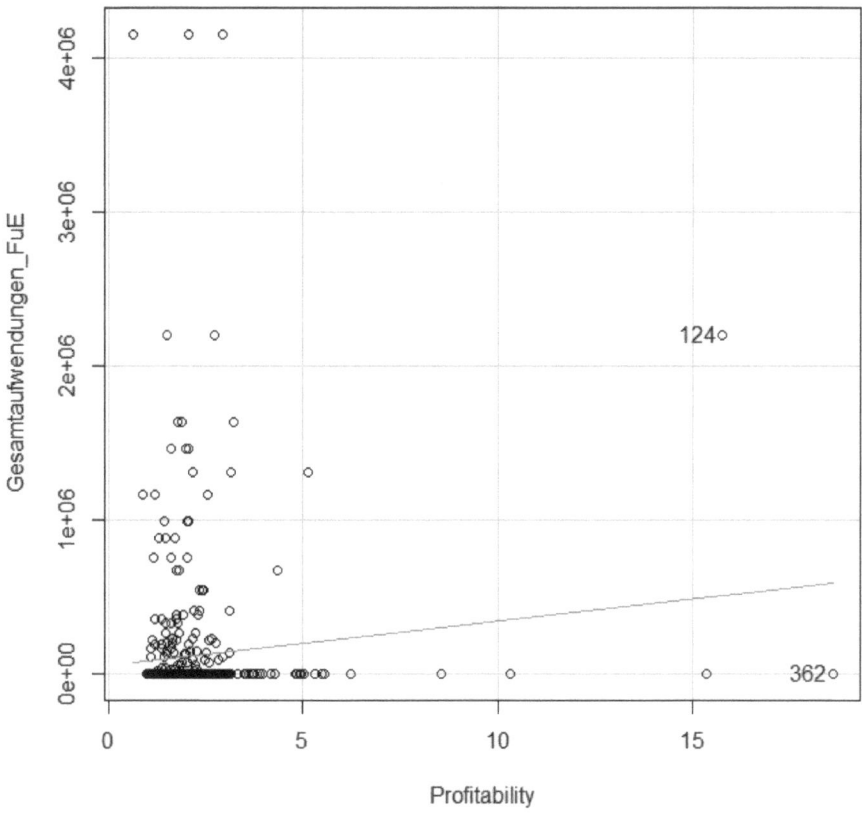

Figure 3: Scatter diagram: Correlation between overall R&D spending and profitability

The green line, which is represents the least square criterion, reveals that there is only a very weak causality. Whether this trend is of significance, is shown by the following correlation analysis:

	R&D expenditure	Profitability
R&D expenditure	1.00000000	0.09528472
Profitability	0.09528472	1.00000000

Table 3: Correlation matrix: Total R&D spending and profitability

Similar to the analyses in Section 3.1.1, with a negligible correlation value of 0.0952, it is obvious that there is no significant connection.

3.1.3 Ratio of cost structure to weighted R&D expenditure

R&D may not only have an impact on the price of a product and consequently on the profitability of the company. A company that invests in R&D may also be in a position to offer the same product at a cheaper price. This is why, R&D investments may lead to a better production process and thus to a more favourable cost structure. The dependencies investigated in Chapters 3.1.1 and 3.1.2 is related to a company's profitability in line with Formula 1. Even though the analysis has revealed no correspondence, there may be a correlation between cost structure and R&D investments. Additionally, it was not clearly identified whether there is any correlation between cost structure and R&D investments. Consequently, the forthcoming examination considers the company's cost structures.

A relationship between the total cost and R&D expenditure would be easier to acknowledge if all companies produced the same product. It would be easy to determine which company can produce at a lowest price and which companies are less efficient. In this case, a connection to the R&D expenditure could be easily identified and researched. However, the sample does not clarify what the companies produce and in what quantities. Therefore, it cannot be determined even within a certain industry using the given data set. In this context, the costs must be related to another aspect. It is conceivable to set the costs in relation to the company's size, for example to the number of employees. However, this does not seem effective, because it is unknown how labour-intensive the specific product is. Most likely, the ratio of costs to revenue seems appropriate, although the economic success of a company plays a role again (this aspect was supposed to be neutralized).

The cost structure in this sense is calculated using the following formula:

$$\text{Cost structure} = \frac{\text{Total costs}}{\text{Total revenue}} \qquad (4)$$

The results can be found in the Column AP of the attached Excel spreadsheet (Appendix 2) and the resulting scatter diagram appears in Figure 4.

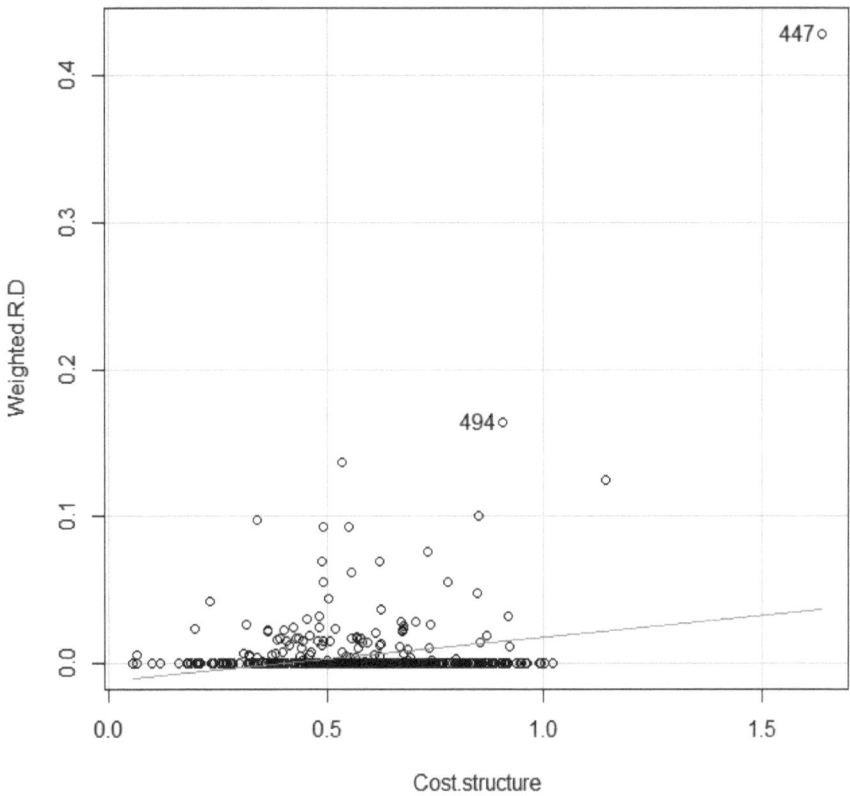

Figure 4: Scatter diagram: Correlation between weighted R&D spending and cost structure

The square criterion reveals that there is only a very weak trend. Whit a value of 0.223, the linked correlation matrix detects an intermediate effect:

	Cost structure	Weighted R&D expenditure
Cost structure	1.00000000	0.2235006
Weighted R&D expenditure	0.2235006	1.00000000

Table 4: Correlation matrix: Weighted R&D spending and cost structure

3.1.4 Ratio of cost structure to total R&D expenditure

For the same considerations as mentioned in Section 3.1.2, this section examines the cost structure and the total R&D expenditure. The resulting figure 5 demonstrates absolutely no connection:

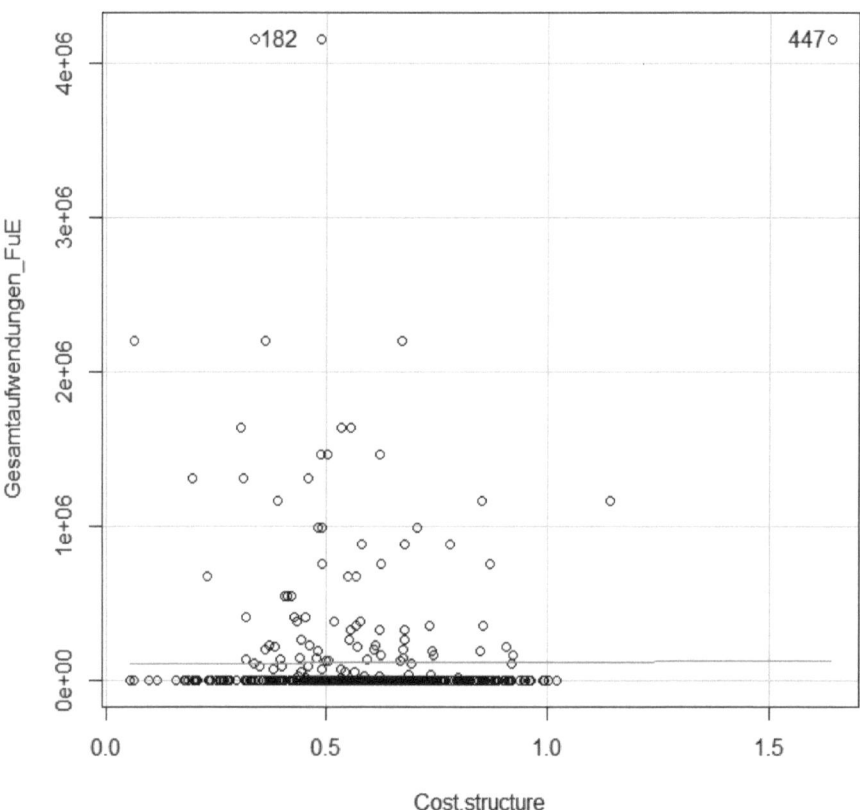

Figure 5: Scatter diagram: Correlation between overall R&D spending and cost structure

	R&D expenditure	Cost structure
R&D expenditure	1.00000000	0.00664276
Cost structure	0.00664276	1.00000000

Table 5: Correlation matrix: Total R&D spending and cost structure

Moreover, the outcome of the correlation analysis with a negligible correlation value of 0.0066 confirms no significant relationship.

3.1.5 Ratio of cost structure II to weighted R&D expenditure

As the investigation has showed no positive relations between R&D investments and the production cost, the research has followed up to find a constraint between cross value added and R&D investments. In the previous investigation (cost structure) the revenue and the related market-success of the company, which is influenced by a number of factors, is included. With the cost structure II formula, using the gross added value, these factors are excluded. In other words, it may be that a company invests in R&D, hence produces at lower costs, but even thought, due to other reasons, has little success in the market. Nonetheless, R&D can be beneficial for this company even it is not working profitable.

$$Cost\ structure\ II = \frac{Total\ costs}{Gross\ value\ added} \quad (5)$$

The cost structure II can be found in the Column AQ of the attached Excel spreadsheet (Appendix 2) and the resulting scatter diagram of this investigation appears in Figure 6.

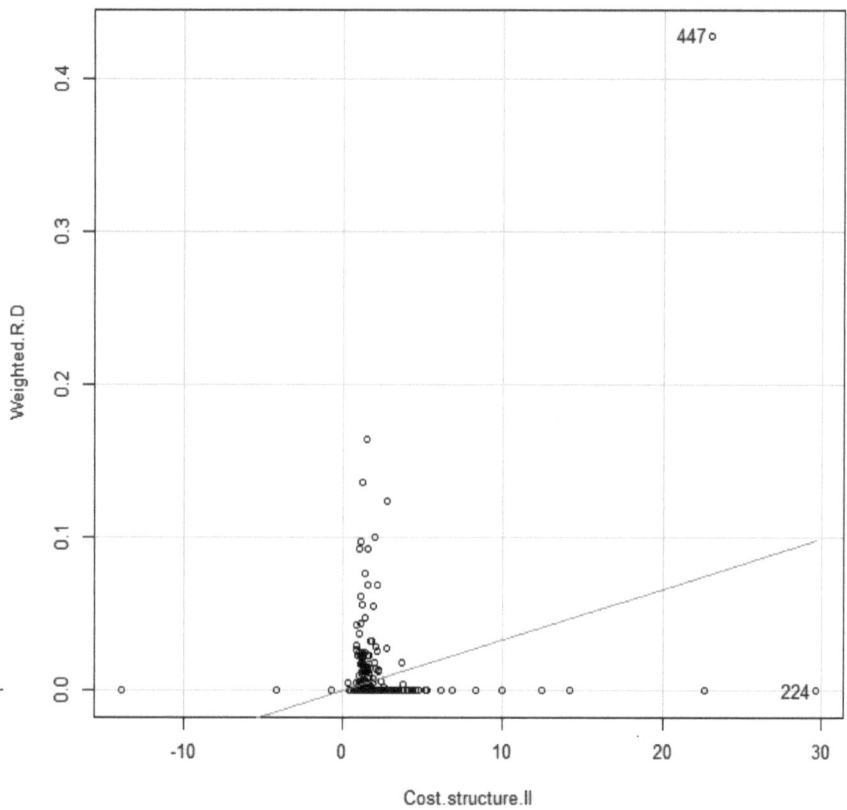

Figure 6: Scatter diagram: Correlation between weighed R&D spending and cost struct. II

The connected square criterion reveals that there is a relevant relation. Whit a value of 0.302, the linked correlation matrix detects an intermediate effect:

	Cost structure II	Weighted R&D expenditure
Cost structure II	1.00000000	0.302742
Weighted R&D expenditure	0.302742	1.00000000

Table 6: Correlation matrix: Weighted R&D spending and cost structure II

3.1.6 Ratio of cost structure II to total R&D expenditure

For the same thoughts as mentioned in Section 3.1.5, this section examines the cost structure II and the total R&D expenditure. The resulting Figure 7 demonstrates a low connection:

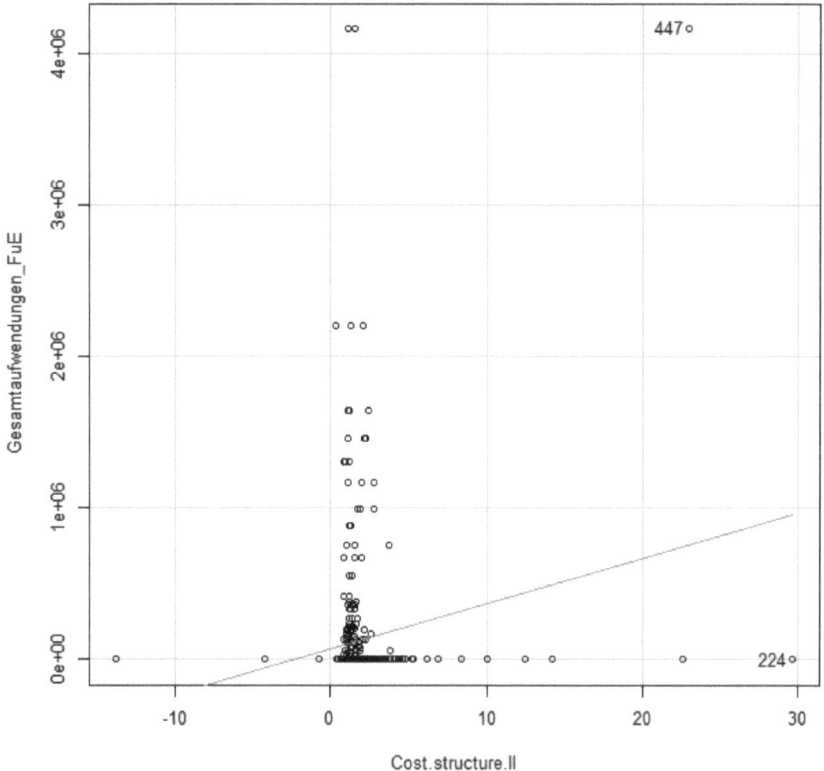

Figure 7: Scatter diagram: Correlation between overall R&D spending and cost structure II

The square criterion in Table 7 with a value of 0.157 implies also a low connection.

	R&D expenditure	Cost structure II
R&D expenditure	1.00000000	0.1570676
Cost structure II	0.1570676	1.00000000

Table 7: Correlation matrix: Total R&D spending and cost structure II

3.1.7 Mean value investigation: T-test for independent samples

The mean value investigation with the R-function called "T-test for independent samples" tests whether the means of two variables differ significantly or not. In this case, whether there are significant differences in profitability between companies that invest in R&D and companies that do not. To perform this investigation, the original data set needs to be modified so that the R&D spending is factorized. In other words, companies that invest in R&D are factored with 1 and companies that not are attributed with 0. Figure 8 replicates the T-test output window from "R".

```
data: Profitability by AnyRaDexpenditure_Faktor
t = -0.36667, df = 135.02, p-value = 0.7144
alternative hypothesis: true difference in means is not equal to 0
95 percent confidence interval: -0.4108754 0.2823499
sample estimates: mean in group no mean in group yes
        2.028639        2.092902
```

Figure 8: T-test for independent samples: Profitability by R&D expenditure

The p-value indicates whether a measured result can also be explained by coincidence. A p-value of 0.7144 is of significance. As a result, the thesis, on which a relationship between profitability and R&D investments exists, has to be discarded. With a probability of 95%, the true difference in mean lies in this interval. That the means of 2.02 and 2.09 are very similar also signifies that there is no relationship between profitability and R&D investments.

In the same way, it was tested if there is a significant difference between profitability and whether or not a company employs R&D personnel. Figure 9 represents this.

```
data: Profitability by RDpersonal_Faktor
t = -0.61527, df = 121.33, p-value = 0.5395
alternative hypothesis: true difference in means is not equal to 0
95 percent confidence interval: -0.4767383 0.2506679
sample estimates: mean in group no mean in group yes
        2.020631        2.133666
```

Figure 9: T-test for independent samples: Profitability due to R&D personnel

As the p-value of 0.5395 is also significant, there is no relationship between profitability and the employment of R&D personnel. Moreover, with a probability of 95%, the true difference in mean lies in this interval. The means of 2.02 and 2.13 are very similar, which is also a sign that there is no relationship between profitability and R&D investments.

In addition, it was tested whether there is a significant difference between the cost structures for companies with R&D investments against companies that do not invest. Figure 10 shows that there is no connection:

```
Data: Cost.structure by RaDexpend_Faktor
t = 0.56216, df = 131.25, p-value = 0.575
alternative hypothesis: true difference in means is not equal to 0
95 percent confidence interval: -0.03333958  0.05981095
sample estimates: mean in group no   mean in group yes
                       0.5825838              0.5693481
```

Figure 10: T-test for independent samples: Cost structure by R&D expenditure

With a p-value of 0.575, it becomes obvious that there is no significance and that there is no relationship between cost structure and R&D investments. Besides, with a probability of 95%, the true difference in mean lies in this interval. The means of 0.58 and 0.57 are very similar. Therefore, no connection was identified between cost structure and R&D investments.

In addition, the same examination shows the relationship between cost structure and whether or not a company employs R&D personnel.

```
data: Cost.structure by RaDpers_Faktor
t = 1.0294, df = 120.8, p-value = 0.3054
alternative hypothesis: true difference in means is not equal to 0
95 percent confidence interval: -0.02289169  0.07247815
sample estimates: mean in group no   mean in group yes
                       0.5845053              0.5597121
```

Figure 11: T-test for independent samples: Cost structure by R&D personnel

Besides, as the p-value is 0.305 and the means are comparable, the thesis, on which a relationship exists, has to be rejected.

Finally, it was tried to find a significant difference between the cost structures II for companies with R&D investments against companies that do not invest, and cost structure II and whether or not a company has R&D personnel. Figure 12 and 13 with p-values of 0,795 and 0,901 and similar means are also rejects the thesis, on which a relationship between cost structure II (cross value added) and R&D investments exists.

```
data: Cost.structure.II by RaDexpend_Faktor
t = -0.25911, df = 144.92, p-value = 0.7959
alternative hypothesis: true difference in means is not equal to 0
95 percent confidence interval: -0.5790569  0.4448270
sample estimates: mean in group no  mean in group yes  1.696197      1.763312
```

Figure 12: T-test for independent samples: Cost structure II by R&D expenditure

```
data: Cost.structure.II by RaDpers_Faktor
t = -0.1247, df = 129.29, p-value = 0.901
alternative hypothesis: true difference in means is not equal to 0
95 percent confidence interval: -0.5699914  0.5023987
sample estimates: mean in group no  mean in group yes
        1.703000       1.736796
```

Figure 13: T-test for independent samples: Cost structure II by R&D personnel

3.2 Analyses for companies which invest in R&D

In the previous paragraph, the whole dataset was basis for the investigation. From 500 companies only 96 are investing in R&D. To achieve a stronger focus on R&D expenditures the data set was reduced. Therefore, this paragraph seeks for the same relations as described in 3.1 using a reduced dataset consisting of 96 companies.

3.2.1 Ratio of Profitability to weighed and total R&D expenditure

Figure 14 shows the regression analyses of weighed R&D expenditure to profitability whereas Figure 15 shows the result for the total R&D expenditure.

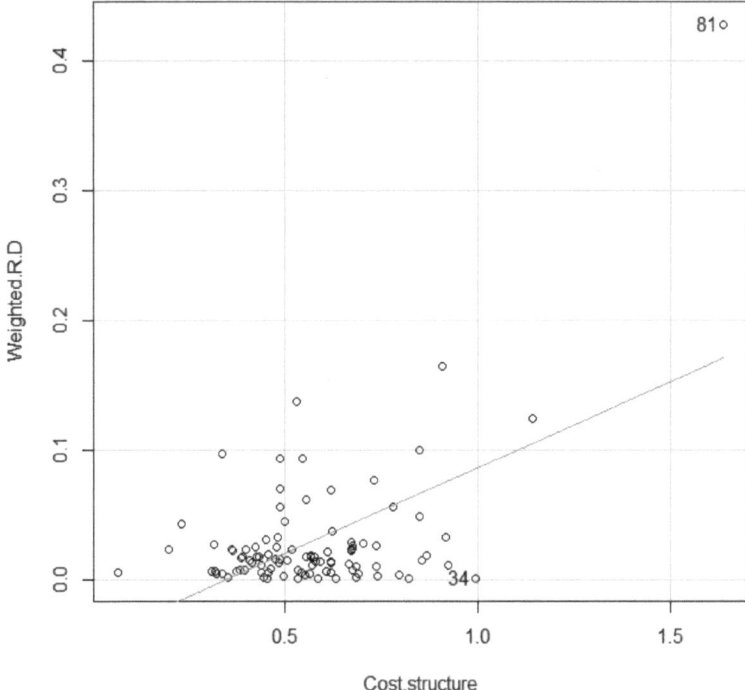

Figure 14: Scatter diagram: Correlation between weighed R&D spending and profitability

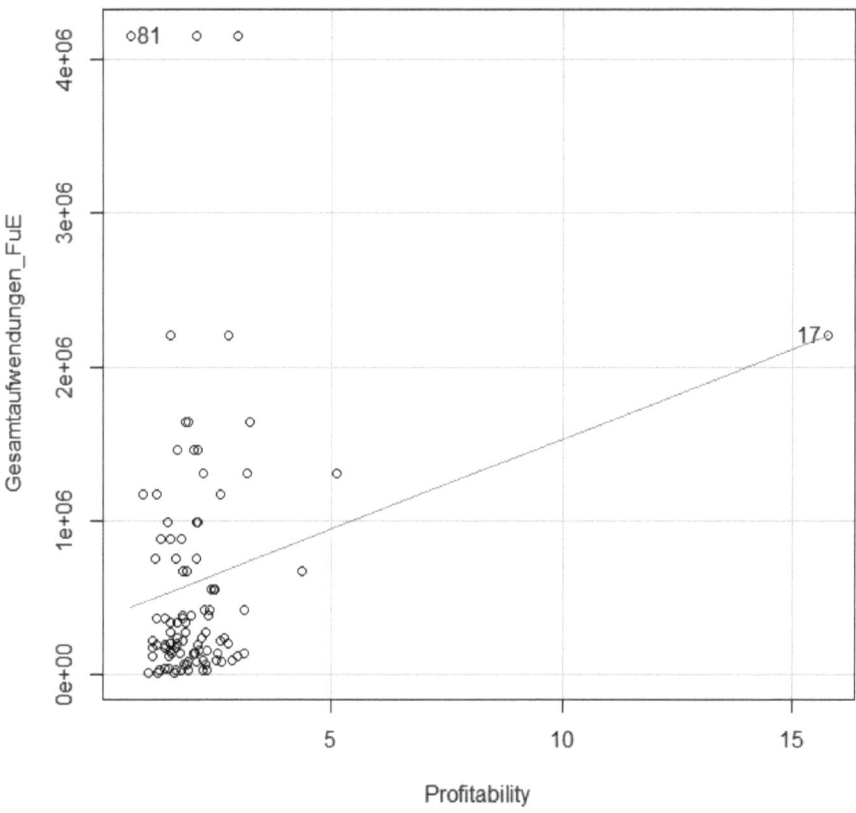

Figure 15: Scatter diagram: Correlation between overall R&D spending and profitability

The square criterion in Table 8 and 9 appears with a value of -0.149, respectively 0.218 and is implying a low or intermediate approximation.

	Weighted R&D expenditure	Profitability
Weighted R&D expenditure	1.00000000	-0.1498217
Profitability	-0.1498217	1.00000000

Table 8: Correlation matrix: Weighted R&D spending and profitability

	R&D expenditure	Profitability
R&D expenditure	1.00000000	0.2180862
Profitability	0.2180862	1.00000000

Table 9: Correlation matrix: Overall R&D spending and profitability

3.2.2 Ratio of cost structure to weighed and total R&D expenditure

For the same consideration concerning the cost structure as described in section 3.1.3 an investigation was done only with the companies investing in R&D. Figure 16 shows the scatter plot of weighed R&D expenditure to cost structure while Figure 17 shows the outcome for the calculation with the total R&D expenditure.

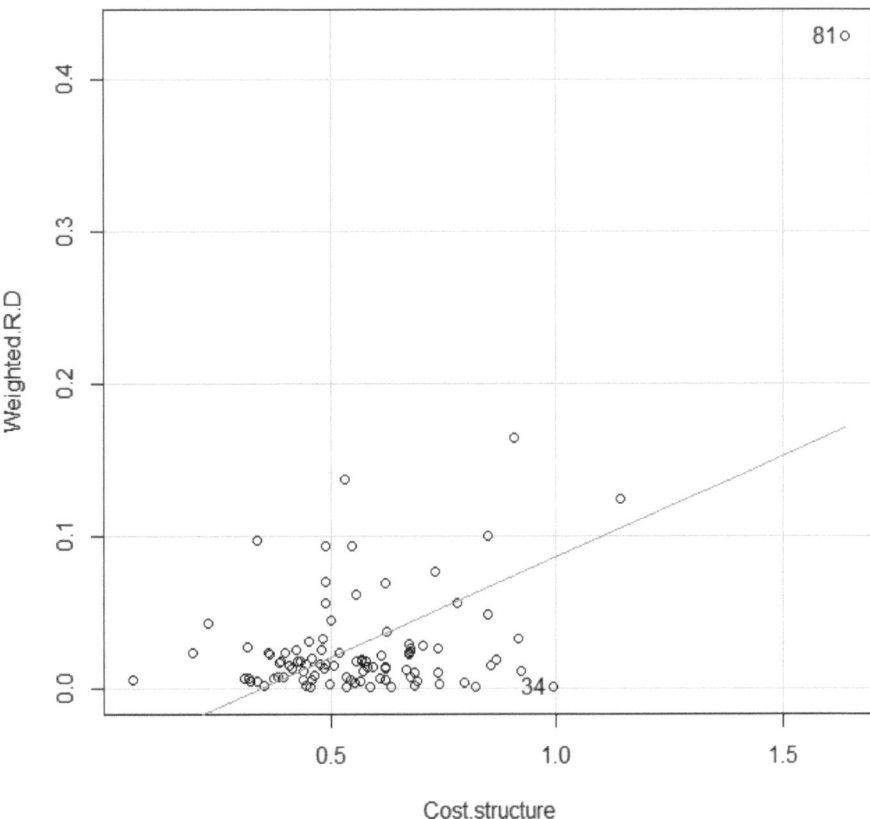

Figure 16: Scatter diagram: Correlation between weighted R&D spending and cost struct.

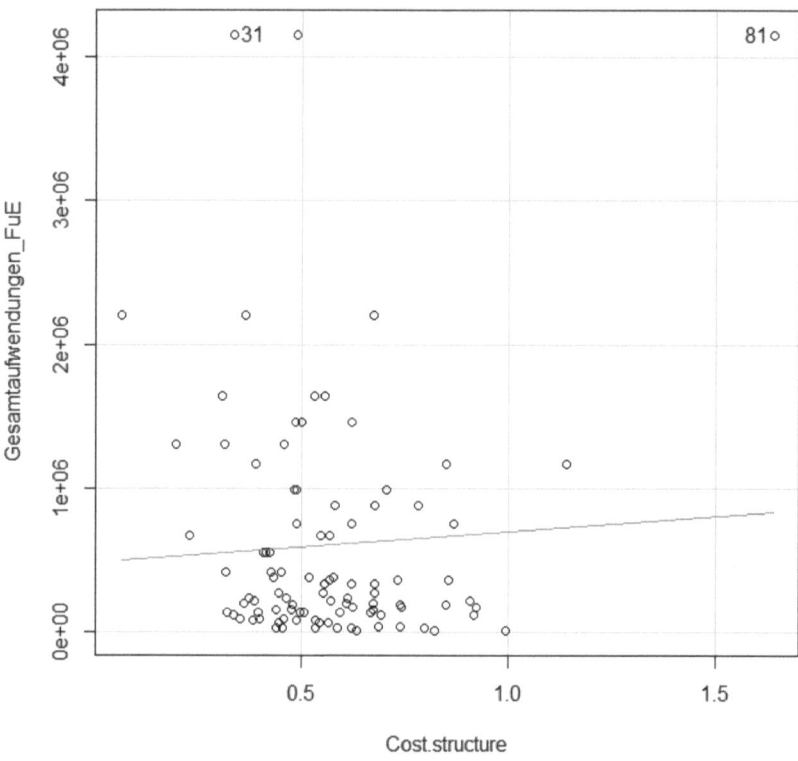

Figure 17: Scatter diagram: Correlation between overall R&D spending and cost struct.

Figure 16 reveals a correlation between cost structure and weighted R&D expenditure for the 96 companies. The correlation analysis in Table 9 confirms with a value of 0.544 a high approximation.

	Cost structure	Weighted R&D expenditure
Cost structure	1.00000000	0.5449862
Weighted R&D expenditure	0.5449862	1.00000000

Table 10: Correlation matrix: Weighted R&D spending and cost structure

In contrast to the finding in Table 10, with a value of 0.05 in Table 11 there is a low relation between total R&D expenditure and cost structure.

	R&D expenditure	Cost structure
R&D expenditure	1.00000000	0.05309767
Cost structure	0.05309767	1.00000000

Table 11: Correlation matrix: Overall R&D spending and cost structure

3.2.3 Ratio of cost structure II to weighed and total R&D expenditure

To complete the research, this section seeks for a relation between cost structure II (formula 5 in section 3.1.5) and R&D expenditure. The Figure 18 pictures the scatter diagram for weighed R&D spending, whereas Figure 19 shows the one for the total R&D disbursement. The strong correlation is highly influenced by company No. 81 which represents an outliner.

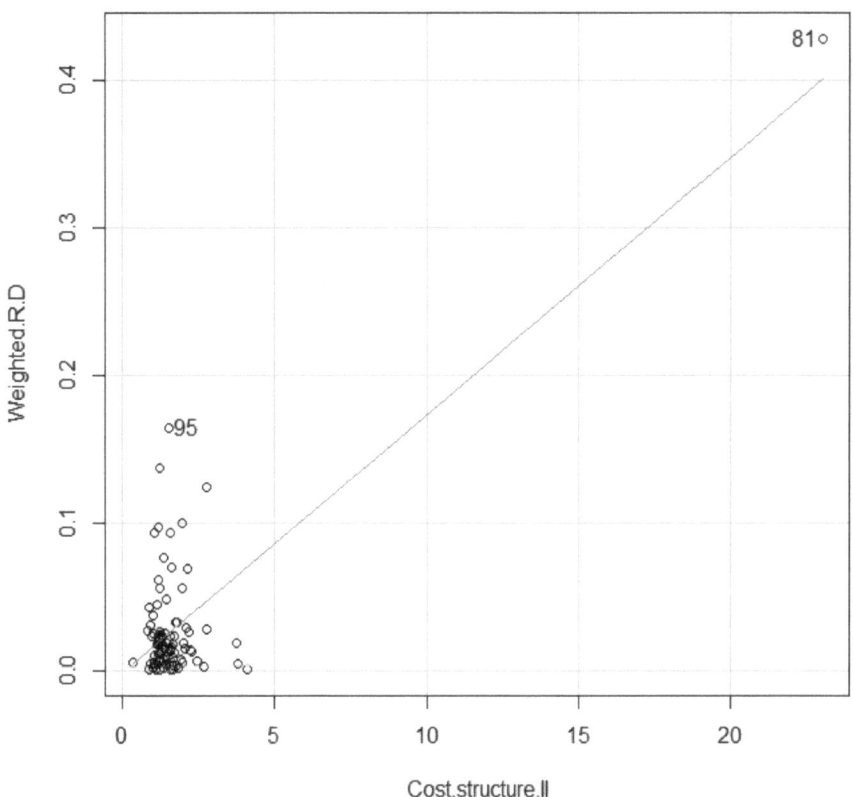

Figure 18: Scatter diagram: Correlation between weighted R&D spending and cost struct. II

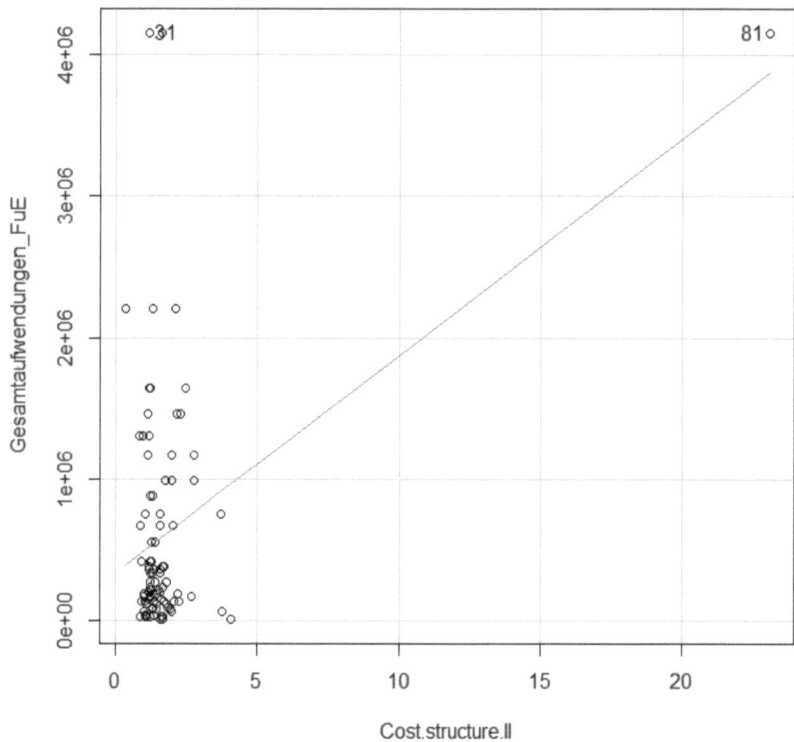

Figure 19: Scatter diagram: Correlation between overall R&D spending and cost struct. II

The related correlation matrixes are looking as follows:

	Cost structure II	Weighted R&D expenditure
Cost structure II	1.00000000	0.7739291
Weighted R&D expenditure	0.7739291	1.00000000

Table 12: Correlation matrix: Weighted R&D spending and cost structure II

	R&D expenditure	Cost structure II
R&D expenditure	1.00000000	0.4166721
Cost structure II	0.4166721	1.00000000

Table 13: Correlation matrix: Overall R&D spending and cost structure II

The value of 0.773 is, according to the definition in Table 1, a very high correlation, while 0.4166 is an intermediate result.

3.3 Analyses for selected branches

In the previous paragraphs, an analysis of all branches was performed. As R&D efficiency can vary from industry to industry, this section aims to look for the relationships for the different branches. If industries have higher investments, higher amplitude of the R&D spending to revenue ratio must be acknowledged. This would prove a correlation between R&D investments and profitability. There might be branches, where companies invest more than in other branches. Certain branches like machine manufacturing or the chemical industry may have higher R&D investment costs than a publisher. The histogram in Figure 20, extracted from Appendix 2, shows the R&D payments in relation to revenue.

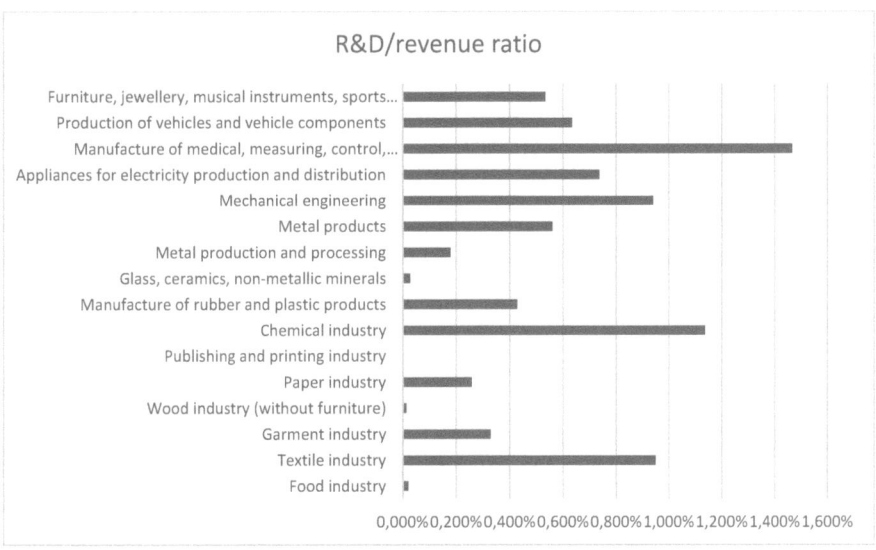

Figure 20: R&D disbursements/revenue ratio of branches

As expected, there is a significant higher R&D investment in relation to the revenue in some branches. The three most significant industries are medical devices-, chemical-, and textile. Hence, these three industries form the topic of further investigations.

The major figures of these three branches are shown in Table 14:

	Number of data sets	Total revenue [€]	Total costs [€]	Total R&D expenditure [€]	Profitability	R&D/revenue ratio
Medical device industry	16	305,626,467	166,309,833	4,481,612	1.838	1.466%
Chemical industry	18	899,819,414	512,619,723	10,238,558	1.755	1.138%
Textile industry	22	468,060,686	236,983,380	4,444,104	1.975	0.949%

Table 14: Figures of branches with the highest R&D/revenue ratio

3.3.1 Medical devices industry

The manufacturing industry of medical devices,-including measuring, control, regulation, and optical instruments, has the index number 33 in the Excel file. The related data consists of only 16 companies, which might not be sufficient for a comprehensive evaluation. The scatterplot proves this:

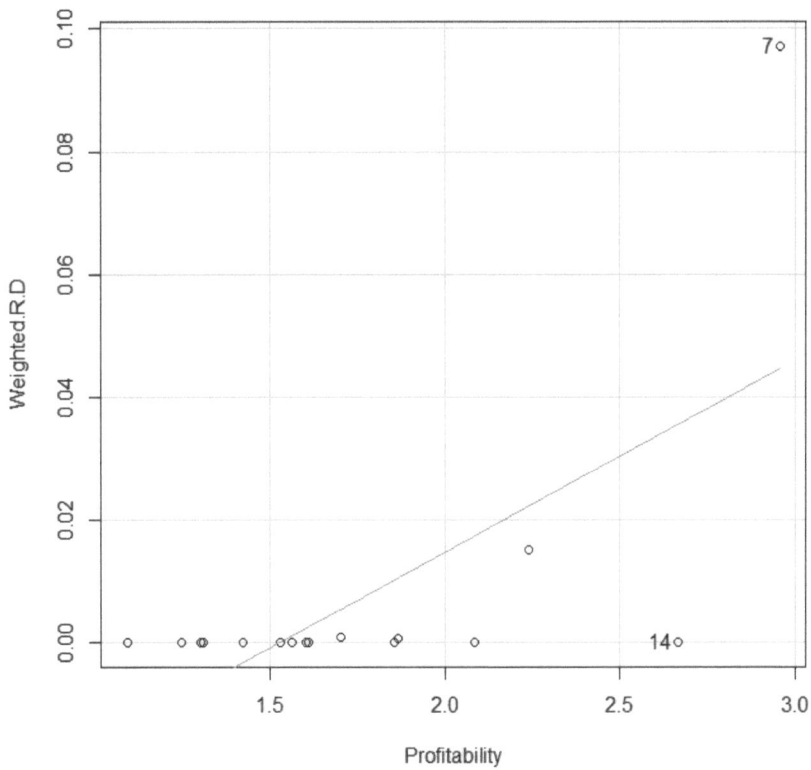

Figure 21: Correlation: Weighted R&D spending and profitability (medical devices)

The highly positive trend finds its cause only in one company. This company (No. 7) invests in R&D and is highly profitable. The second profitable company (No. 14), on the contrary, does not invest. Therefore, the relationship is meaningless. Whit a value of 0.661, the correlation matrix in Table 15 indicates a strong connection between profitability and R&D expenditure, which is also a meaningless statement.

	Profitability	Weighted R&D expenditure
Profitability	1.0000000	0.6616391
Weighted R&D expenditure	0.6616391	1.0000000

Table 15: Correlation matrix: Weighted R&D spending and profitability (medical devices)

Owing to a small number of data sets, no significant statement can be achieved with the T-test, which, therefore, was not further applied.

The examination of the relationship between profitability and the total R&D expenditure (equivalent to the investigation in Section 3.1.2) shows the same meaningless results:

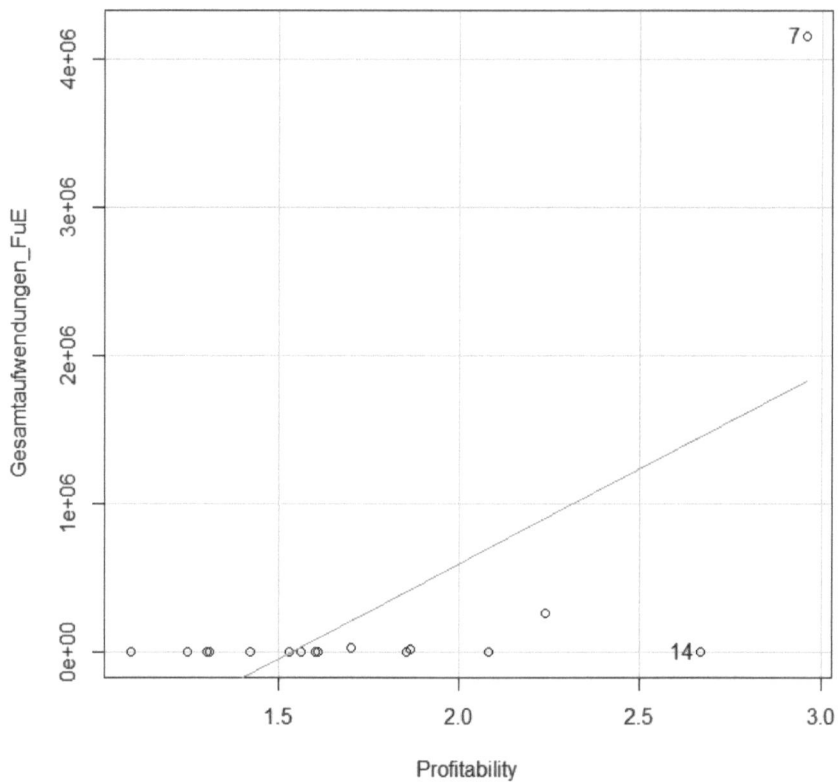

Figure 22: Correlation Overall R&D spending and profitability (medical devices)

	R&D expenditure	Profitability
R&D expenditure	1.00000000	0.6410195
Profitability	0.6410195	1.00000000

Table 16: Correlation matrix: Total R&D spending and profitability (medical devices)

3.3.2 Medical devices industry without outlier

The examinations in Section 3.2.1 lacked an extreme outlier. The company represented by data point No. 7 invests heavily in R&D and is highly profitable, while the second profitable company does not invest at all. Consequently, the examinations in Section 3.2.1 without data point No. 7 are repeated hereunder.

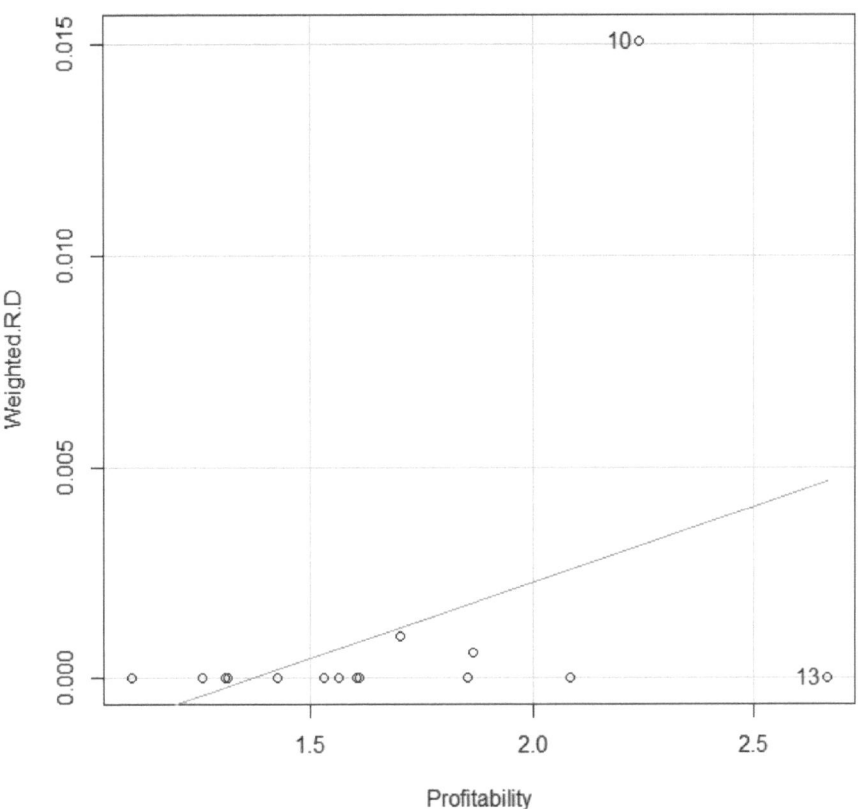

Figure 23: Correlation Weighted R&D spending to profitability (without outlier)

There is still a positive trend, but this trend is substantially weaker. Accordingly, the correlation matrix still shows a weaker connection:

	Profitability	Weighted R&D expenditure
Profitability	1.0000000	0.3847023
Weighted R&D expenditure	0.3847023	1.0000000

Table 17: Weighted R&D spending and profitability (without outlier)

As expected, the scatter diagram and the related correlation matrix for the total R&D expenses for profitability, also display a positive trend and correspondence.

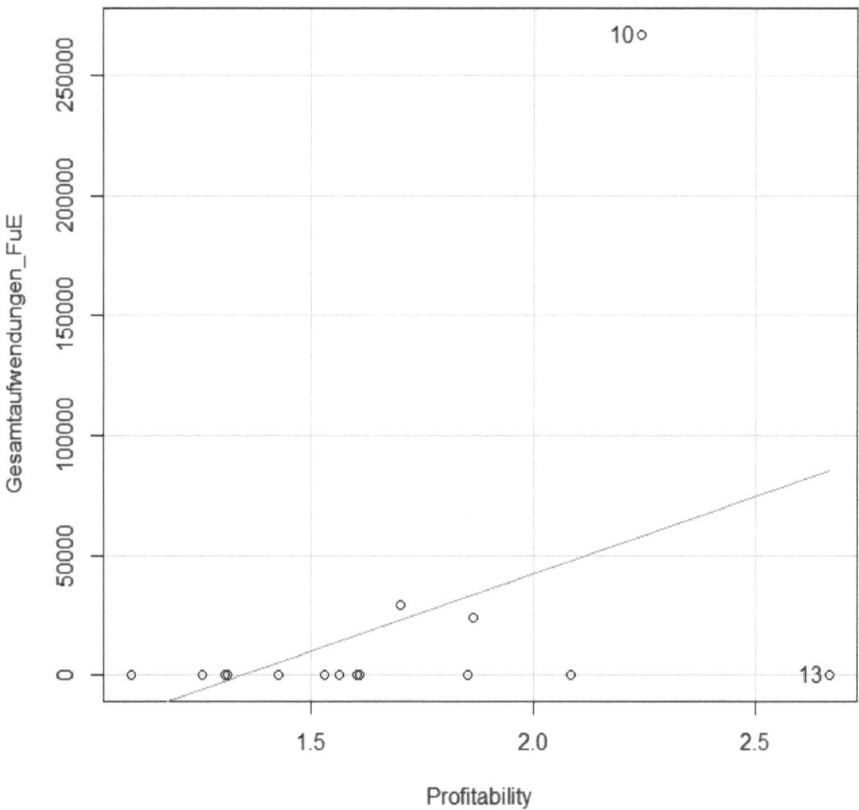

Figure 24: Correlation: Overall R&D spending and profitability (without outlier)

	R&D expenditure	Profitability
R&D expenditure	1.00000000	0.3917253
Profitability	0.3917253	1.00000000

Table 18: Correlation matrix: Total R&D spending to profitability (without outlier)

However, a dataset comprising only 16 companies is not sufficient to identify meaningful relationships. One could argue that the company represented by dataset No. 10 is now an outlier. Excluding this company most likely would not give better (more reliable) results. If one excludes this company, there is also the risk of the investigation being manipulated until the desired results appear. As a result, the investigation was stopped at this point.

Even if the analyses were done in the same way for the chemical and textile industries, it would be of no use showing and describing the results for these industries. The chemical industry consists of 18 data sets, the textile industry, of 22. The examination for the chemical and textile industries found similar results as to the one for the medical industry. Even if a correlation was found, it could only be explained by coincidence, as this section has uncovered.

3.4 Results

For to full data set the following can be concluded:

- Where there are enough data sets, only a very weak relationship between profitability and R&D expenditure can be identified. It makes no difference whether the R&D costs are weighted or not.
- The examination of the relationship between weighted R&D and cost structure shows an intermediate effect, while the relationship between total R&D and cost structure is negligible.
- The investigation with the cost structure II formula, taking into account the cross added value, discovered a relevant correlation.

For the research performed with the data set of companies investing in R&D the following was exposed:

- There is a low for weighted and an intermediate relation for the total R&D expenditure to profitability.
- There is a high correlation between cost structure and weighted R&D expenditure, while there is a low connection among cost structure and total R&D disbursement.
- A very high connection for cost structure II to weighted R&D spending and an intermediate link to the total R&D spending was found.

The approach to consider the branches with the highest R&D investments revealed the following: The medical devices industry was identified as having the highest R&D expenditure to profitability ratio. Hence, it was chosen for further examination. This examination revealed a strong relationship. However, the scatter diagrams has clarified that this relationship is coincidental. For industries with the second and third highest R&D investments, similar results were found. Table 19 in this paper summarizes the results and the interpretation of the correlation coefficient of the whole study.

Test Sample	Pearson's product-moment correlation coefficient	Interpretation of coefficient
All companies		
Weighted R&D / Profitability	-0.05463883	low
Total R&D / Profitability	0.09528472	low
Weighted R&D / Cost structure	0.2235006	intermediate
Total R&D / Cost structure	0.00664276	negligible
Weighted R&D / Cost structure II	0.302742	intermediate
Total R&D / Cost structure II	0.1570676	low
Companies invest in R&D (96)		
Weighted R&D / Profitability	-0.1498217	low
Total R&D / Profitability	0.218	intermediate
Weighted R&D / Cost structure	0.544	high
Total R&D / Cost structure	0.053	low
Weighted R&D / Cost structure II	0.773	very high
Total R&D / Cost structure II	0,416	intermediate
Medical devices industry		
Weighted R&D / Profitability	0.6616391	(high)
Total R&D / Profitability	0.6410195	(high)
Medical dev. industry without outlier		
Weighted R&D / Profitability	0.3847023	(intermediate)
Total R&D / Profitability	0.3917253	(intermediate)

Table 19: Overall summary of correlation matrix results and interpretation

The Table 20 collates the insights derived from the T-test investigation.

T-test for independent samples	p-value	Interpretation of thesis
Profitability by R&D expenditure	0.714	no relationship thesis is wrong
Profitability by R&D personal	0.539	no relationship thesis is wrong
Cost structure by R&D expenditure	0.575	no relationship thesis is wrong
Cost structure by R&D personal	0.305	no relationship thesis is wrong
Cost structure II by R&D expenditure	0.795	no relationship thesis is wrong
Cost structure II by R&D personal	0.901	no relationship thesis is wrong

Table 20: Overall summary of T-test results and interpretation

4 Conclusion and outlook

The R analysis of the full dataset has clearly showed that there is no constraint between R&D expenditure and the key performance indicators such as revenues, or profitability, or success at company level. Moreover, the research for a positive connection between costs of a company and R&D spending were of no success. Even though, the research with the companies who invest is R&D has found a high and a very high approximation the result was voided by contradictory findings in similar investigations. Additionally, the investigation has suffered from outliners in a too small data set. That means if a connection was found, it could only be explained by coincidence. Also the research for selected braches revealed no reliable causality.

Accordingly, the thesis of this investigation "Research pays and leads to better company profitability" needs to be disregarded.

Consequently, we can confirm the theory of Schmeisser (described in Section 2.1), that there is no causality between R&D expenditure and the overall company success for SMEs in the processing and mining industry.

4.1 Recommendation

To follow up on this scientific question "Does research pay?" we would rather recommend a bottom-up approach then a top down calculation. This approach could be the measurement of the total benefit of an R&D department for a given company by considering all the R&D projects undertaken in the company. That means, taking all the net present values (NPV) of all the business cases (BC) of the entire R&D project portfolio. A business case is updated constantly during project evolution to prove the reasonability of the project.[18] In big companies, it can be done even at the portfolio level by calculating the average/median of all the BC's of the R&D project portfolio. This would facilitate answering the question "Is R&D beneficial?" for a given company. In case, this data were available for the lion's share of companies operating in industries like the automotive industry, a generic answer to the question can be provided for this branch. Assuming that this data were available for all DAX enterprises, we could state a heuristic for Germany. This approch seems to be unrealistic for the time being as these figures have a high degree in confidentiality for the companies.

---

[18] Rf.: Mulcahy, R. (2013), pp. 120 - 121

Besides, the way how R&D initiatives are managed differs across organizations, industries, and countries. Despite that within the frame of a harmonized and professional PM (e.g. PMI Standard), the needed techniques are available, it seems impossible to acquire this data. That is because of different PM standards like PMI, Prince or IPMA and because these techniques (streamlined BC calculations at the portfolio level) might not sufficiently deploy in a wide array of companies.

Naturally, this approach would work in a perfect world, which means where the R&D department is performing only research and development and not any other engineering activities such as customization or customer service. Moreover, the same calculation rules for all the BC's like the same discounting rates need to be secured. Another weak point of this approach is that a BC is based on assumptions. Besides, there is the manner in which the ideas and innovations are incorporated into the current product or services of the company. This is a crucial point especially for product modifications and diversifications. This brings us back to the initial problem that the success factors range across a wide product- service lifecycle and are dependent on too many factors in the entire business.

4.2 Related Studies

Several studies from other branches show a positive correlation between R&D expenditure and company performances. For example, D'Este (2002) in a study of Spanish domestic pharmaceutical firms during the period of 1990 - 1997 identifies that, among manufacturing, R&D and marketing, building new product development capability is particularly associated with enhanced firm performance. In a study of small metal-working firms in Northern Italy, Gurisatti et al. (1997) find that success depends on developing new competences of "a cumulative character" and in-house innovative capability. Other studies (e.g. Tripsas 1997; Petroni 1998; Deeds et al. 1999; Delmas 1999; Lazonick and Prencipe 2005) also reveal that a firm's innovative capability is a critical factor for the firm's evolution and survival in light of external competition and change. The more innovative a firm is, the more it possesses dynamic capabilities and with that the related performance.[19]

Niels Nolsøe Grünbaum and Marianne Stenger have done another comparable study of small and medium-sized manufacturing enterprises operating in volatile environments. The authors

---

[19] Rf.: Wang, C. (2007), p. 17

examine a wider field of dynamic capabilities. In the resulting paper, they state: "The findings reveal a positive relationship between dynamic capabilities and innovation performance in the case companies, as we would expect. It was however, not possible to establish a positive relationship between innovation performance and profitability. Nor was there any positive relationship between dynamic capabilities and profitability."[20]

In the last three years, the companies in their study saw a decrease in profit before net financials (i.e. EBIT) in the interval of 78% to 133%, a decrease in gross profit in the interval of 15% to 60% and a decrease in net profits in the interval of 81% to 140%. The ratios for the latest annual report (i.e. 2011) illustrated a return on assets in the interval of 3% to -9.8% and a return of equity in the interval of 1.3% to -65.4%, thus revealing a rather disturbing development.[21] Therefore, Grünbaum and Stenger even found a negative correlation in their studies.

The different studies give contradictory results, thereby reinforcing the idea that, if there is causality, it cannot be identified owing to the disturbing factors in this foggy research environment.

4.3 Summary

Even though there is a dearth of proper data and consequently no sustainable empirical evidence that research is useful, the authors of this assignment want to highlight their opinion.

Research pays and is beneficial.

This is especially true for companies where R&D is managed wisely and where development is pushed forward through certain processes. That says, companies which have professional PM techniques deployed; most importantly BC method above. The NPV in the BC is updated constantly during the evolution to secure a return on investment. In case the NPV becomes a negative figure, the project, and as well the idea and the related innovation, needs to be stopped or even terminated.[22] A mature PM to push innovation and to manage the related dynamic capabilities has a supportive impact. This thesis is corroborated by the findings of Salomon and Hauschild. Particularly incremental innovations are positive influenced by milestones tracking, scheduling, and formula reviews. In contrast, radical innovations are

---

[20] Grünbaum, M. (2013), p. 68
[21] Rf.: Grünbaum, M. (2013), p. 78
[22] Rf.: Taschner, A. (2008), p. 15; this assignment is not going to give any further explanation about BC and the related key figures or even PM techniques.

benefit from the breakdown structures, organized communication, and cost management in the frame of PM.[23]

Having the light bulb example in mind, we can surely claim that had it not been for R&D and the associated innovation, or people who are unhappy with the status quo, we would still only have candle light.

---

[23] Hauschildt, J. (2011), pp. 316 - 323

List of appendices

Appendix 1: Original Excel data set

Appendix 2: Modified Excel data set

Appendix 3: ITM checklist

Editor's note: Due to their size, appendices 1 and 2 are not included in this editon. They can, however, be requested free of charge at the publishing house. To request the Excel data sets please contact us: info@anchor-publishing.com

List of references

Hauschildt, J./Salomo, S. (2011): Innovationsmanagement, 5th Edition, München

Schmeisser, W./Mohnkopf, H./Hartmann, M./Metze, G. (2008): Innovationserfolgsrechnung, 1st edition, Berlin Heidelberg

Amberg, M./Bodendorf, F./Möslein, K. (2010): Wertschöpfungsorientierte Wirtschaftsinformatik, 1st Edition, Berlin Heidelberg.

Zimmer, Marco (2015): „Statistical Analyses -Introduction into R" Skript Research Methods SS 2015 from the MBA Program at the FOM Hochschule für Oekonomie & Management, Essen.

Taschner, A. (2008): Business Cases, Ein anwendungsorientierter Leitfaden, 1st Edition, Wiesbaden.

Mulcahy, R. (2013): PMP Exam Prep, 8th edition, USA.

Wang, C./Ahmed, P. (2007): Dynamic Capabilities: A Review and Research Agenda, from: The International Journal of Management Reviews, 9(1) ,Middlesex,2007, pp. 31 – 51.

Grünbaum, N./Stenge, M(2013): Dynamic Capabilities: Do they Lead to Innovation Performance and Profitability?, from: The IUP Journal of Business Strategy, Vol. X, No. 4, Roskilde, 2013.

Busse von Colbe, W./Laßmann, G. (2013): Betriebswirtschaftstheorie: Band 1 Grundlagen, Produktions- und Kostentheorie, 5th edition, Berlin Heidelberg.

List of internet references

HIL (2015): "The History of the Incandescent Lightbulb"
URL: http://inventors.about.com/library/inventors/bllight2.htm (22.06.2015)

Fernandez, E. O. (2009): "Statistik mit SPSS"
URL: www.uni-goettingen.de/en/111790.html (22.06.2015)

Appendix

Appendix 3: ITM Checklist

Topics	Issues critical for success	Comments / suggestions
General economics	Economic relevance of the topic	As R&D is a crucial aspect of entrepreneurship, it must be important for the general economy. Innovation leads to technical developments and consequently to economic growth, enhanced convenience in life and better living standards. Using the example of a light bulb, it can be said that without R&D and innovation, we would still only have candle light.
Strategic management	Relevance of the topic concerning - Securing existence - Competitive advantages - Tying up resources - Sustainability - Risk - Dynamic capabilities	The topic is closely related because strategic management decisions are influenced by companies' R&D efficiency and there resulting outcome. R&D efforts mainly serve to secure existence, help develop a competitive advantage and defend it, secure resources, and enhance sustainability. R&D projects can involve enormous risks. It can lead to a total loss of investment or can be detrimental to reputation. As a major framework in strategic management, the dynamic capability discussion is highly concerned with the innovative capabilities and related R&D efficiency of a company.
Marketing	Advantages and disadvantages of the proposition regarding - marketing measures - external impact - general productivity - internal/external marketing	Marketing must be an important aspect of R&D, innovation, and their efficacy. The marketing department of a company can provide inputs (external impact). It knows best what customers want and can inspire the R&D department to offer innovative products or services. Additionally, marketing uses techniques (6P, internal/external marketin etc.) to create demand in the customer, thereby helping to bring the product into the market and increase sales. In other words, in case of improper marketing, even the best innovation would not sale and the company's R&D efficiency would be recognized as low.
Financial management	When choosing appropriate financial terms - criteria's that have to be considered	Since the paper is a quantitative analysis of financial figures, the relevance of this area of knowledge cannot be ignored. To increase or even secure the likelihood of success of R&D projects companies should utilize business cases in order to decide whether to start a project or not. The calculation of the NPV, the internal rate of return,

		- risks and safeguarding measures - impact of externalities	payback time and peak exposure by making a cash flow estimate and using a dedicated discount rate helps to ensure R&D payout. As this assignment and other investigations indicated, an explicit causality between R&D expenditure and EBIT or revenue cannot be found, even though this relationship is there. Innovations can result in obvious or hidden externalities. Taking the electro car, this technically could enhance the use of nuclear energy. The resulting financial risk needs to be considered as well, not just at company, but also on general economic level.
Human resources management	Personal consequences		The connection to the HR function comes via the management for innovation projects and their related personal consequences. Typical HR management tools and methods include the following: staffing management plan, resource calendars, team building, team performance assessment, project performance appraisals, issue logbook, responsibility assignment matrix, resource-breakdown structure, and resource histograms. These PM tools help to secure project success, thus enhancing R&D efficiency.
Business law		- legal topics - steps to ensure legal certainty	In general, if the company has a legal department, one representative should be part of the project team when it comes to project selection. Innovations can have internal (personal) and external (environmental) legal consequences. These consequences are needed to be within the frame of law and assessed according to their legal impact. Moreover, patents, property rights and certifications need to be considered.
Research methods		- sources of information to be used in order to stay up to-date	The dataset comprises the cost structure and balance sheets of 500 German companies in the field of processing trade and mining. It represents a smooth and anonymized microanalyses. It is a cross section investigation. For statistical analysis, MS Excel and the "R" programming language have been used. As this assignment seeks to solve a real world problem by quantitative analysis of data, it can be described as business research.
Soft skills / leadership qualities		- managerial requirements - forms of leadership	Innovation projects need to be initiated, planned, executed, monitored, controlled and closed. This requires a project team and a team leader with sound project management skills and leadership qualities. Since R&D projects are uncertain, a collaborative leadership style is preferred.